THE LITTLE PURPLE BOOK

Leadership

A Series of Tips ... But No Tricks

Because there aren't any!

Ali Esshaq

aliesshaq@gmail.com

CONTENTS

Foreword

It may be difficult to recall the essentials when you find yourself launched into the thick of it.

Or ...

When you are up to your ass in alligators ...It may be difficult to remember the idea is to drain the swamp!

This is not one of those mumbo-jumbos, pseudo-philosophical books on Leadership. *The Little Purple Book* is a book you will actually use, read, refer to again and again.

The Little Purple Book shows you how to adapt proven practices for your own life and your organization. What works for me, will work for you. I'll show you how to create, train and manage; to bring out your best, the best in your Team and your organization. *The Little Purple Book* gives you practical tips; *but no tricks ... because there aren't any!*

Okay, let's be perfectly clear on this:

The purpose of *The Little Purple Book* is to introduce you to me!

Or rather to my way of helping the *Best* get *Better* and how I help make *Winners* into *Champions!*

The *noble intent* is to provide you with thought provoking insights to encourage you to explore your options.

The goal of *The Little Purple Book* is to entice *you* to seek the professional services I provide.

The reality is for a lot of you, this is all you will ever need. *The Nobel intent.*

Far too many of you already know it all – or think you know it all. Personally, I find this slightly annoying ...

> *"People who think they know everything* are a great annoyance to those of us who do."*

> Isaac Asimov

For those of you who found enjoyment in the above ... *"Welcome!"*

"I have neither the time nor the inclination to explain myself to a man ..." well, for those of you that get it; you know where I'm headed.

What's your biggest challenge?

I can help you! BUT first, take a quick read of the contents provided here. I hope you will find value and inspiration to ask better questions, seek more information and when you are ready ... let's talk. I don't have the answers, but *You* do! And I can help you find them!

The Little Purple Book is intended to stimulate a much more informed and intelligent debate about the way forward and what you as a forward-thinking Leader, need to do to *improvise, adapt and overcome!*

Currently the business world is being driven by what is referred to as the *4th Industrial Revolution.* This revolution is unlike any other. The speed at which business must adapt is unheralded. This indicates that you must embrace change. Change has always been and will always be, the driving force for all businesses.

Forward-thinking Leaders must have insights on what they believe their future holds. They must also envision the future not in the context of the here-and-now, but in the direction and magnitude of where they need to be. Preparing now must be built on a solid foundation. Failure to build on a solid foundation is a recipe for disaster.

I understand your success, perhaps even your survival, depends on making fundamental **changes** to your business, to your operating model.

What is clear is you cannot afford to focus only on short-term steps in your transformation journey. A focus on the long term is essential, including the following:

- Redefining strategic direction and priorities
- Significantly shifting the operating model that drives improved efficiency by simplifying the operation's core
- Establishing sound partnerships and pursuing select acquisitions to quickly achieve the additional capabilities the new offerings will require
- Embracing *digital* to realize benefits across the business, including new services, enhanced experience, greater process agility, and improved cost efficiency
- Upscaling the skills and competency levels of the employee base, and
- Revisiting company culture and governance

You must learn to improvise, adapt and overcome. Your mantra should be *Adapt or die!*

Within these contents there are some *lessons learned,* I hope you will find valuable.

If you are just looking for some key pointers, they're in here. I am sharing with you the business expertise I have accumulated over the past 50 years, things you need to know to reach your goals and be more successful.

For those of you who choose to read the contents in their entirety, along the way you will learn decision making, risk management, a little about finance, a whole lot about planning and I will touch on marketing.

Also, hopefully, we will have some fun – just to keep it interesting!

So now you know, I am actively engaged in what you do.

And I am good at it. Damn good.

So *WHY* am I doing this? Giving you my Tips.

Well, it's complicated. As of this writing, my daughter is in college and she asked me what she should do after she graduates to make a living *(I thought she would just join me and continue doing what I do.)*

But if she wants to do something else, great.

I just want her to have access to the things I have accumulated over my life-time to help her be successful at whatever she wants to do.

So, this *The Little Purple Book* is it.

Now, you have access to the same information.

Since I am writing this for her, I thought I may as well share it with other people who are *smart enough* to seek guidance when the time is right.

Why this? Why now? And why me?

I answered those for you.

Another *WHY* question you should as is:

Why will this not work for me?

It will not work for you! If you do not do your part. Your part is to learn, ask questions, challenge the status quo. I'll show you how to do these things. I can teach you *HOW* because I have already done it.

You must *DO IT* because you want to.

If you have what it takes to make it!

I do things differently.
I will teach you the Leadership and tactical skills you want and need to be a more successful business Leader and a better person.

And a final *Why* reason. I like the way I feel when someone says to me, B*ecause of you, I didn't give up!*

Ali Esshaq

Semper Fi

> Professionally and personally, I subscribe to the United States Marine Corps Leadership Philosophy. Which I have adapted to provide your business with those advantages.

In my world ~ There are two Leadership objectives:

The primary objective is to accomplish the mission (objectives.) This requires a goal-oriented approach. A Leader must identify long-term goals for the team and the short-term steps the organization needs to take to achieve those goals.

The secondary objective of Leadership is to take care of your Team. This objective requires empathy on the part of the Leader to make sure the needs of those on the team are looked after and given diligent care.

LEADERSHIP

There are thousands of articles about Leaders and Leadership, and countless thoughts on what Leadership is and isn't. Not to mention a constant stream of new articles, blogs and information. With so much going on, it becomes more important than ever to stay focused on what's most important.

> *"If your actions inspire others to dream more, learn more, do more and become more, you are a Leader "*
> **John Quincy Adams**

Being a Leader is to inspire. A Leader is not a savior but more like a spark that incites!

> *"Professional Leaders need to regain their concentration on the art and science of Leadership through personal development and they should establish requirements for training that directly supports core tasks for all Team members."*

Great Leaders never die; their speeches, their legacy transcends and is measured by the way they affected their society, country and sometimes the world.

My Definitions

Leadership ~ The action (or ability) of leading a group of people or an organization.

Leader ~ The person who leads a group of people or an organization.

Management ~ The administration of a group of people or an organization.

Manager ~ The person who administers a group of people or an organization.

"Managers do things right. Leaders do the right thing."

— Warren G. Bennis

"One does not manage people ... the task is to lead people. And the goal is to make productive the specific strengths and knowledge of every individual."

Peter Drucker

I place very high importance on understanding the above. Understanding the difference in the roles of a Leader versus a Manager; is paramount to your success. The expectations are different, the methods are different. A good Manager should exhibit good Leadership skills. A good Leader must have excellent Management skills. The two are not exclusive. They are complementary skills.

The essence is the focus:
– Leaders do the right thing
– Managers do things right!

Learning is as important, as what you learn.

Improve yourself, do things in the future that are beyond your current possibilities.

It is exciting and fulfilling.

Develop an insatiable curiosity to continually improve your Leadership skills.

Keep learning, keep getting better! Never stop learning!

Things to learn:

- Listen
- Get help

- Listen
- Take the Initiative
- Listen

Trust

Trustworthiness (Integrity) is the single greatest quality for creating Leadership.

Trust is a game changer.

> *"We don't judge people. We validate them for who they are, not for who we want them to be. That's how everybody wants to be treated. Besides, manipulation never works." ...*
>
> **Robin Dreeke**
>
> *"The Code of Trust: An American Counterintelligence Expert's Five Rules to Lead and Succeed."*

To inspire trust, put others first.

CHAPTER 1

Leadership Competencies

I subscribe to the philosophy of Leadership principles and Leadership traits.

Go ahead and "Google" Leadership competencies ... I'll wait. You will get about 8,090,000 results, including *Most important; Top Ten; The 28; etc*. on the first page. Wow, over 8 million hits.

So why do I say there are 11 Leadership principles and 14 Leadership traits? And what makes me the *one* out of over 8 million you should listen to?

Well, it ain't me.

It is the proven system. For over 242 years has been refined to create the best Leader s!

I have adapted the verbiage to suit you, to help us to communicate better; however, the *Competencies* – those *Principles* and *Traits* contained herein; well, they have withstood the test of time and I am smart enough to recognize they are exactly the way forward in today's world.

Many of the traits and characteristics commonly found in Leadership competency frameworks, at first glance appear to be a comprehensive framework for Leaders. Including values *(principled, integrity)*, cognitive skills *(inquiring, thinking)*, interpersonal skills *(caring, enthusiasm, communicating)*, diversity components *(tolerance, respect, empathetic)*, and change orientation *(open-minded, risk taking)*.

You are facing a rapidly evolving and complex future. It is crucial that Leadership is well defined, described and taught. Part of our challenge includes establishing a common language for discussing Leadership concepts.

Defining Leadership is an important first step toward establishing how it should be conducted within an organization.

However, a simple definition is insufficient for describing the nature, boundaries, contexts, and desirable manifestations of Leadership. Hence, the need to discuss **Competencies.**

Familiarize yourself with the following to help us to effectively communicate:

Be technically and tactically proficient

Maintain a prominent level of competence in your specialty. Your proficiency will earn the respect of your Team.

> *You have a specialty. It is that one thing you know better than most people. It may be the one thing you have studied the most. Whatever it is – make sure you keep it up to date. Make sure YOU are the ONE who is sought out whenever the subject comes up.*

Know yourself and seek self-improvement

Evaluate your strengths and weaknesses. An accurate and clear understanding of yourself and a deep comprehension of group behavior; will help you determine the best way to deal with any given situation.

Know your team and look out for their welfare

Know your Team and how they react to different situations.

This knowledge is gold.

Having knowledge of your Team's personalities will enable you, as their Leader, to decide how best to employ and challenge each member.

Keep your team informed

An informed Team performs better and, if knowledgeable of the situation, can carry on without your personal supervision. Providing information inspires initiative.

Set the example

Set the standards for your Team by personal example. Your Team will watch your appearance, attitude, physical presence and personal example. If your personal standards are high, then you can rightfully demand the same of your Team

Ensure the task is understood, supported and accomplished

Before you can expect your Team to perform, they need to know what is expected of and from them. Communicate your instructions in a clear, concise manner, and allow your Team a chance to ask questions. Check progress periodically to confirm your expectations are being properly accomplished.
Set an objective or goal; provide the *Why* and allow your Team to develop the *How*. Provide any support they need.

Train your Team as a Team

Train your Team with a purpose and emphasize the essential elements of teamwork and realism. Teach your Team to train and operate as a team. Be sure all Team members know their positions and responsibilities within the team framework. Take opportunities to *cross-train*. Mix it up occasionally, it will challenge your Team and help them develop new skills and in turn will build their confidence in themselves and the other Team members.

Make sound and timely decisions

Rapidly estimate a situation and make a sound decision based on your estimation. There's no room for reluctance to decide. Decide and then revise it when required. Your Team respects a Leader who corrects mistakes immediately.

Develop a sense of responsibility in your Team

Show your Team you are interested in their welfare by giving them the opportunity for professional development. Assigning tasks and delegating authority promotes mutual confidence and respect between the Leader and the Team members.

Employ your Team in accordance with its capabilities

Successful completion of a task depends upon how well you know your Team's capabilities. Seek out challenging tasks for your Team, but be sure your Team is prepared for and can successfully complete the assignment.

Seek responsibility and take responsibility for your actions

Actively seek out challenging assignments for yourself. Seeking responsibilities also means you take the responsibility for your actions. You are responsible for everything your Team does or fails to do. Stick by your convictions and be willing to accept justified and constructive criticism.

CHAPTER 2

Behavior

Your Team expect their Leader to act like *Leader*. Always maintain your behavior. You are always being observed.

Never lose your cool.

It's important to always act as if you are in control. Maintaining your behavior is more than just keeping up appearances. It's a reflection of your mental discipline and how much you control your mind and soul.

If you don't, you just showed you couldn't keep your mind and emotions in check. If you cannot during regular times, what will happen when you're faced with extreme stress or fear?

Courage

Our first thought when we hear this word is courage in the face of danger. Yes, of course and moral courage is equally important.

Moral courage to step in and say when something is wrong, when it's an unpopular thing to do.

Do you have the moral courage to challenge a senior when you know they are wrong?

Moral courage means making the right decision when it may be unpopular.

Decisive

Better a decent plan executed now than a perfect plan executed tomorrow. The smartest Leader is worthless if he cannot be decisive in his decision-making. The two words have similar roots. We have all seen Leaders who are indecisive. Decisions need to be made in the real world. Waiting allows the situation to get worse.

Poor Leaders try to come up with a *perfect plan*, which is useless. *Perfectionists* are just indecisive people who have the luxury not to act quickly.

Dependable

This means exactly what it says: Your Team wants to trust you will always be there for them.

This is particularly true where ideas and taking risks matter.

Endurance

Physical endurance for Leaders is obvious.

Physical fitness is key to enable endurance for the physical challenges of the job.

But there is also emotional endurance, the mental will to keep going when you think you can't.

You cannot afford for your Team to see you weary or even appear to be thinking about slowing down.

Your Team doesn't have the luxury of letting up. They have children and other daily responsibilities they must tend to.

Your Team looks to you for their inspiration, to keep going when it is tough.

You must set the example. Take care of your physical endurance to enable your mental endurance.

Inspire your Team.

Enthusiasm

You must be enthusiastic if you expect your employees to be enthusiastic!

Enthusiasm is contagious, but so is negativity.

Attitude is everything.

Determination

Grit

Firmness of purpose; passion, perseverance, and stamina.

It is *something extra, it* separates the most successful from the rest;

Adapt and overcome obstacles

Fearless, not fearful; make the tough decisions, now; every moment spent deciding is time lost on getting it done.

Manage emotions, feel them – but manage / control them – never decide when your emotions are not in your control.

Trust yourself, look at decisions from every possible angle, and when the facts don't present a clear alternative, believe in yourself and your ability to choose; go with what looks and feels right.

Patience

Overdeliver.

Pay attention to the details – mind numbing data is valuable information when you put in the effort.

Take the high road, never stoop down to others lower levels – instead raise them to the higher level.

> *NEVER argue with a stupid person, they will wear you down to their level and then beat you on experience!*
>
> *NEVER wrestle with a pig, you will both get dirty – BUT the pig*

likes it!

Never make or offer an excuse – be accountable for the results.

Solve the problem.

Initiative

You must always have a bias for action. Keep moving. Don't wait around for someone to tell you what and how to do it. Assess the situation, the intent, and make a move.

This is a critical trait.

Initiative not only works to solve the problem at hand, but more importantly, can prevent it from worsening or allowing other problems to manifest due to inaction.

Integrity

A Leader must have the moral authority to lead, govern, and discipline; the foundation of which is based on integrity.

Without integrity in your Leadership, your Team will lose their own integrity.

As a Leader, you must set the example with integrity so it sets the environment for everything else.

Judgement

Judgement is key for decision-makers with personnel issues and in handing down discipline. It is important to always keep the welfare of your Team in mind to steer your conscience.

Even when mistakes occur, *and they will*, you can at least know you were thinking in the best interest of your Team.

Your judgment is critical, you can cost your company money, its future, and cause countless harm.

The welfare of your Team matters the most.

What is the goal of your company, are your employees taken care of so they are the most productive as they can be?

If your judgment rests on the value of your company's mission and the care of your employees, then most of your decisions will be good ones.

Justice

Leaders must have an intense sense of justice. Without it, one cannot effectively lead. A Leader's character must be impeccable, never wavering in the face of uncertainty. When a Leader does not ensure an environment where justice is the rule, breakdowns in behavior will inevitably occur.
Justice gives a Leader the moral high ground to enforce discipline.

Conversely, a CEO cannot expect his company to thrive, for his employees to give it their best if they do not feel justice exists in their workplace.

This means talent and work ethic gets people promoted, nothing else.

This means employees are treated with justice, and employees feel safe and know they are judged according to the quality of their work and nothing else.

Employees must trust if legitimately wronged, they will be heard and justice will be rendered.

Knowledge

You are the subject matter expert in your organization.

Are you? Is your talent trusted?

Are you the Leader your Team wants to follow?

Are you the Leader who provides a rich environment where your Team may be successful?

Know what is necessary to be a Leader. Be a Leadership expert.

Better yet, know what is needed to be a trusted and respected Leader.

Be that Leader.

Loyalty

Loyalty to your Team and to your principles.

Loyalty should never be confused with looking the other way and ignoring a situation out of a misplaced sense of loyalty to one another.

As a business Leader, you should be loyal to your company and the values you claim to espouse.

Loyalty goes in both directions – Loyalty up to the organization and Loyalty down to your Team.

Tact

You will get more bees with honey than with vinegar. It is always better to build someone up; using tact will do that.

People will make mistakes, correct them, but no need to crush them if you plan to keep them around.

Be careful how you speak to people. It's important.

Unselfishness

Your people come first.

Always remember that.

Would you eat, sleep, or take any amenity before your own children?

No, you wouldn't. At least you wouldn't if you cared enough.

Then why would you do it with your people?

Everything thing you do should be with that in mind.

Never make a comfort-based decision.

Think of others first, those who you are entrusted to care for and lead.

As a corporate Leader, ask yourself, are you thinking of quality of the product or service you offer?

Are you keeping the profits at the expense of your employees who put in countless hours making the company successful?

WARNING: SALES PITCH

I will give you the tools, but to move forward, you must have it in your heart. You must want it. You must COMMIT.

I'm talking about leading people in the most chaotic, stressful environment there is.

I can teach you how you can make yourself a better Leader and perhaps a champion!

You can demand respect but you won't get respect unless you've earned respect.

That's a very important part of Leadership- *Learning How to Earn Respect.*

One day you may oversee millions of dollars' worth of assets and have many people depending on you.

I can help you to be a better Leader and overall it will make you a better person - ready for any situation.

I can teach you how to think on your feet and basically to decide at the point of friction whatever the situation may be.

IF – *YOU have what it takes!*

People want Leaders, and from day one; I help make better Leaders, not only in business but also in your personal life.

I can help you to make the difference.

Leadership is also about having a vision; it's not about just the here and now. It's about where you need to be and creating the vision for your Team and being able to inspire them to focus on it and to do the best job they can possibly do.

END   SALES PITCH

PART TWO

Change

Why Change?

Change in business is inevitable. *YOU EITHER CHANGE OR YOU WILL NOT BE IN BUSINESS.*

Organizations have more projects, less time, and change is constant. Ensuring Change Leadership is integrated with Management activities is important to achieve desired results and planned business outcomes.

Since change is constant, why are there so many issues when trying to implement something new?

Transforming your organization is and it will never be; a perfectly smooth process.

No matter how committed the senior Leaders, well-thought-out the strategy nor the organizational buy-in; breakdowns will happen. However, after shepherding many change-management projects, I firmly believe a commitment-based approach to change management leads to greater results faster and with the fewest problems in implementation.

After all, your business, your company is a group of people working together to accomplish an agreed objective. When something changes, your people's emotions are affected. They may feel defensive, fear, suspicion or even hostility if you change what they agreed to!

What changed?   Factors may be internal or external.

An external event may be something like when the business environment changes ... hopefully, you have in place the systems required to exploit this change. *If you don't, then you are in a reactive mode ... behind the curve and in a situation where you will be forced to make the required changes faster and at a lot higher cost than those organizations who envisioned the change and prepared for it!*

This is indicative of poor strategic planning; and it is <u>the primary responsibility of Leadership</u>.

An internal event may be anything which effects the status quo - the normal or usual way - the organization operates. A natural event like a flood, fire, earthquake ... any one of these or similar events will result in a change to the organization.

Proper disaster planning is <u>the primary responsibility of Leadership.</u>

What about the unexpected loss of a key employee? In today's environment, there is always the chance someone may receive an offer-they-can't-refuse!

Proper retention planning is <u>the primary responsibility of Leadership</u>.

What if a key employee passes away?

Proper succession planning is <u>the primary responsibility of Leadership.</u>

What if one of your team develops a better way to do something? Say, increase production by 20%. That will effectively change the requirements on both sides of the process. From the supply chain to the delivery model. While this is a good change, it presents some significant issues requiring change!

Did your organization plan for this? Is R&D aligned with Operations? Is Procurement on board? Is Marketing and Sales pre-

pared?

Proper planning ... you guessed it ... <u>the primary responsibility *of Leadership.*</u>

The difference between successful and extinct organizations is the recognition and successful execution of the transformative process. Embarking on a transformation is more than just deciding to do something different or trying something new.

It requires examination, planning, and execution. And a lot of communication!

Transformation is not a *once-and-done* event. A one-time makeover is the dying gasp of an organization! Change must become normal and an accepted part of your organization's way of doing business. Successful, sustained organizations are those which are continually transforming themselves.

Did you notice my emphasis on *Leadership?* I cannot stress the importance of the difference between Leadership & Leaders versus Management & Managers.

DO NOT confuse the two.

HOW TO CHANGE.

Communicate the need for an organizational change.

- • The objectives *and benefits* must be clearly expressed in terms all can appreciate.
- • Convince them of the need.
- • Instill a sense of urgency.
- • Define the value – demonstrate the benefits!
- • Define the risk of not acting.
- • Define what is in it for them!

The importance of effective communications cannot be over stressed. Leadership must make a clear statement of the objectives and benefits of the change. Smart Leaders will provide the *WHY* the change is required. The WHY must be presented in such a manner as to instill confidence in making the change. Pointing out the WHY should also address the potential risk of failure to change, and the cost of failure to change. The WHY must also convey a sense of urgency, specifically demonstrate how much is being lost each hour/day/week /month by NOT making the change is costing and how much more benefit will be recognized when the change is the new normal. Stress the benefits to the individuals of the change. Make it personal to make it important!

Communication is *the primary responsibility of Leadership.*

Managing resistance.

It is *a normal human emotion* and requires:

- Communications
- Participation
- Support
- Negotiations

It Starts at the TOP

If you lead primarily with what you learned in the past ...
YOU ARE ALREADY IRRELEVANT.

Adapt or Die   An organization that does not adapt to its environment ... WILL DIE.

Make *comprehensive changes* or *YOUR COMPANY ESSENTIALLY DIES.*

FACT: *SOME LEADERS ARE STUCK IN THE PAST.*

FACT: **Too many managers + not enough LEADERSHIP = YOU FAIL.**

I am a firm believer in:

"Those who fail to learn from history ... are doomed to repeat it."

We must always be looking forward, but we should understand our history so as not to repeat the mistakes of the past. I have seen too many instances where people continue to pursue wrong courses of action because they do not take the time to think critically about what has happened in the past.

Use *lessons learned*! Yours and anyone else's!

As you develop your strategy for moving to the next level; evaluate your lessons learned and ensure you're not on a collision course with a known issue! Always evaluate your current efforts with your long-term strategy. By constantly evaluating your current plans (tactical) against your long-term strategic plan, (vision) you will have the opportunity to adjust whichever is required.

> "*A strategic company adjusts its course in appropriate time since it is impossible to foresee when the surrounding world will force certain changes to occur. The defensive company is forced to implement the same changes at a later stage, at a much higher cost.*"

Lead from the FRONT!

> Which is more effective?
> "Follow me!" or
> "What I need for you to do is …"

Leadership means you are always *out front.* Not because you are the boss, but because you have a sharp vision of where you need to go. Making a change to your organization requires YOU *show-the-way.* By being visible to everyone in your organization, by speaking to each person you meet, by helping others to see the change is vital to them – this is what I mean by:

It starts at the Top.

Five Phase Change Process

> The process is simple:
>
> Phase 1: Engage the C-suite
> Phase 2: Build awareness
> Phase 3: Educate and Train
> Phase 4: Practice Continuous Improvement
> Phase 5: Create Reward and Recognition

The Five Phase Process effectively manages all facets required to successful implement the Change Management Plan.

Imagine announcing a new program which produces higher profit margins. Imagine announcing penetrating a new export market. Imagine announcing a new partnership with a global power player.

There is a disconnect between how well organizations think they are managing their projects and how well they're doing.

There is a need to *skill-up* managers; especially their skills to lead change, manage conflict, resolve grey issues, and in communications. It is time to for those who only have technical project management skills, to develop their *soft skills*.
The actual process itself is simple, follow these five phases.

Phase 1: Engage the C-suite

Unless your people believe you are genuinely committed to the change, the process will fail.
Create a senior team to oversee the change process
Including a commitment in the organizational vision
Align long-term and short-term goals
Create and communicate a company-wide message

Let's explore – *Create a Senior Team to oversee the change process* –

This does not mean you look around the table and appoint some heavy hitters to *manage* the change process. Nothing could be further from the objective!

Why? – You ask?

First – Your *Heavy Hitters* are also your most active (busy) productive and engaged Team members. This means they will only be able to contribute a limited amount of time and effort to overseeing the change process.

This is NOT the time to overburden your heavy hitters! If you ask each to recommend a trusted Team member (or 2!) they are comfortable with assigning this additional workload; then they your *heavy hitters* can oversee in their role as a coach/mentor – making themselves highly visible as strong advocates for the change initiative. This enables the organization to see additional Leaders who have COMMITTED to making the Change a reality. The more faces of championing Change ~ the better!

Second – Identify those personnel most impacted by the change initiative. Those with skin-in-the-game!

Recruit them, persuade them and appoint them as Champions of the change. Solicit their input and especially their criticism! Provide them with a reporting structure directly to the TOP not just to the overseers.

Why? You ask?

These are the key resources to enable change. And they are also the Leaders of the *resistance movement!*

Fact is any change will generate resistance. Chalk it up to human nature or any other reason. Trust me; *there will be resistance.*

Managing resistance is a key factor to success. Your *oversight* Team will never be informed of any resistance due to the human element. Survival is at stake here. There is always an impact from any change. That is the very reason to make a change. To make an impact. And someone is going to feel the impact. And they are going to react. It is much better to have those who *feel* the impact involved from the earliest stages, especially in the development of the *Why Change* stage.

So why does there need to be a *direct reporting structure* to the TOP and the overseers?

Speaking truth to power is not in the best interest of the status quo. Again, human nature at work. However, if the information i.e. suggestions, questions, concerns, etc. are presented – <u>unfiltered</u> – to the oversight Team, it allows consideration of alternate points of view. Here is the key to success and the key to managing resistance. You can only manage what you measure. Honest reflection of concerns, questions, suggestions or ideas will encourage more of the same. The more ideas the better! The more questions … the better! The more discussions … the better!

Why? You ask?

Your heavy hitters got to their positions by being better than the others at doing things *by the book!*

How could you possibly imagine they would perceive it to be in *their best interest* to change what got them where they are?

NO WAY!

This is the true source of the resistance movement. Not open disagreement nor dissent. It is through their lack of *Championing* the change that the initiative will wither and die.

They can afford to wait it out! In fact, depending on their tenure, it may be their best course of action!

So, how does *direct reporting structure* to the overseers' aide in enabling the change initiative?

Provided the Senior Team includes Top Management (See: *It starts at the Top*) and there is a firm commitment (with buy-in) then the direct reporting – unfiltered – will shine a light on those issues which are identified by those most impacted by the change initiative. *THAT* is the true source of identifying where opportunities exist to modify the change initiative. Take advantage of those most important insights made available by those with skin-in-the-game!

For instance:

Let's keep it simple. Let's change the buying process. After discussions, we have determined we have identified an opportunity to reduce our cost by entering a long-term arrangement with one of our vendors. Traditionally, we have purchased the resource by tendering. The proposed method (the *Change*) will do away with the tendering process and cut cost significantly. Sounds like a great idea, right?

Let's identify those players impacted by the proposed change:
- Buyers

- Procurement
- Procurement Manager

Well, of course they are impacted.

What about other internal players, like clerks or secretaries? How about warehousing? Shipping / receiving? Logistics? How about Contracts / Legal? How about Risk Manager?

Well now, that surely expanded our list in a hurry!

- What about external stakeholders? Other vendors? And their supplier? How are they impacted?
- What about customers? How will this change impact them?
- What about other external concerns? Who else may be impacted?

The people with skin in the game will identify these types of issues – **IF they are involved** in the *Why Change* stage … and these are invaluable insights! When issues are raised early, the opportunity to assess and address concerns are respectfully discussed and decisions are based on merit and value – then the change process will incorporate those Champions required for success.

If you think this is complex, remember, this is a *simple* example of a minor change to an existing process; wait till we undertake a New initiative!

This should reinforce your understanding of *It starts at the Top* is critical to success.

Phase 2: Build awareness

Buy-in must occur within the various levels of the organization.

Once management commitment is secured, the next step is to assess the gap between the current state and the desired state.

This includes gathering feedback from your staff and managers;

which requires *managing resistance to change.*

The first thing we need to do is rewrite the first sentence above! Buy-in must occur within the various levels of the organization – needs to be:

> *Buy-in must occur within <u>ALL</u> levels of the organization; and with full awareness on impact to external concerns.*

While we may have identified a need for change – and there are always going to be needs for change – the assessment of the WHY and the HOW are paramount to success. Don't just change; make a change which is aligned with the future state envisioned.

Think about this: a new regulation prohibits sale of petrol and diesel fuels. As a car manufacture; what changes do you need to make? WOW! That's a good one! (Take a look at what Germany is facing!)

In our example, a simple change in the buying process, we noted the impact on a wide variety of players. We did not address what impact would occur to the systemic processes. For example – signature authority for procurement. If a buyer has signature authority limited to say 50,000, then a procurement manager has a limit of say 250,000 and over requires Management approval. The contract value under the new scheme is more than 1,000,000 ... who is responsible for evaluation and recommending approval? *Ah ha!* The existing process must be modified! Does it result in two processes ... one for *normal* buying and one for the new deal? Or does it require a change in the Approval process only? Does the contract approval process address purchasing? Is risk management approval required? How are Quality audits affected? These issues are of vital importance; therefore ... *Build Awareness* is a critical-to-success factor.

Phase 3: Educate and Train

Change requires educating, training, encouraging and supporting your Team. This must include everyone. Long-term changes cannot be made in your company without the commitment and support of management, so it's critical to train them in their role as well, including:

- Evaluating their staff's attitude and abilities
- Coaching staff in the principles and skills
- Supporting, encouraging and rewarding

Keeping with our simple change in the buying process example – educating everyone. This may require only a quick meeting to familiarize key players with the new way of doing things … or it may require a workshop with detailed explanation of the various nuances required.

How do you determine what education and or training is required?

Solicit feedback from the Team.

Also, it is a promising idea to have representatives from other business areas participate. There may be some valuable insights offered to address accomplishing those goals.

Evaluate those managing the change also. There may be a need to educate them. This may require a specialist or it may be as simple as ensuring they have the knowledge and are comfortable with implementing the change. Either way, better to assess and prepare as needed.

Phase 4: Practice Continuous Improvement

It's impossible to implement change without reviewing the processes, procedures, systems and standards at the heart of the way a company does business; both internally and externally.

Involve staff at all levels and in all areas of the organization, they provide a significant opportunity for employee engagement in the process.

Congratulations! It is done! You have successfully implemented the change! The cost savings are increasing profit margins ... Top management is pleased and life is good.

Matter of fact – it is so good; Top Management is going to implement more changes effective very soon!

Are you ready?

By continuously reviewing systems, processes and the standard way of operating, you will develop the skills and more importantly, the mind set to perform change management as a normal way of conducting business.

Your organization should be encouraged to identify *What's next?*

The world is constantly changing, the environment your organization operates in is constantly evolving and new opportunities are just around the bend. Be ready, anticipate change and embrace it! Become known as a Leader in making progress through effectively leading and managing change.

Phase 5: Create Reward and Recognition

What Leadership says will only carry as much weight as what Leadership rewards. Financial incentives are only one form of recognizing acceptable behavior. Creating an environment of recognition is equally powerful. Private and public praise, promotions, acknowledgment and awards are all part of the change process.

The secrete?

Pizza!

Okay, so it's a little simplistic – but you get the idea.

How about a nice announcement on LinkedIn for the Team accomplishment? Or Facebook, Twitter, Instagram?

Why not?

Share the recognition wide and far! Celebrate achievements!

These will contribute to Team building and develop a sense of community that makes your organization looked upon favorably. In the overall scheme of things, great people want to work with great Leaders and great Leaders make wonderful places to work.

More pizza!

Change Management

Change occurs in three steps:

Unfreezing   The unfreezing step consists of the process of getting people to accept the change.

Moving   Involves getting people to accept the new, desired state

Refreezing   Aims at making the new practices and behaviors permanent

Change derives from two forces, those internally driven and those externally imposed.

Participation is defined as *the active involvement of all employees* in the decision-making process of an organization.

THIS IS THE POINT OF FAILURE. Leadership's failure to implement a process where influence is shared among individuals who are hierarchically unequal.

The lack *of participation of employees* is a major cause of disappointing results with organizational change. Employees must believe their opinions have been heard and given respect and careful consideration.

There is empirical evidence of the communication process and organizational change implementation are inextricably linked processes.

Communication is highly important in the successful implementation of the change processes, because it is used as a tool for announcing, explaining and preparing the change.

THE CHANGE MESSAGE SHOULD ADDRESS:

- The **need for change,**
- the **benefits of the change**,
- the **appropriateness of the change**, and
- **confidence in the capacity** of individuals and the organization to undertake and implement the change.

The message should also vigorously demonstrate there is **Top Level Leadership's** firm and unwavering commitment and support for the change and the benefits associated with the change.

Top level Leadership's commitment and support must be apparent to each employee and _top-level management_ must not allow mid-level _managers or supervisors_ to dilute the message or detract from its importance to each employee.

Top level Leadership must put a face on the message and that face must be known personally by every employee. By the way – the more faces the better!

Most change programs fail due _to lack of energy_ devoted to _internal public relations_ to help those affected by change to better understand it. Again, for an organization to be effective, it needs to cultivate an atmosphere of reliable and valid communication, which provides for integration and employee commitment to the organizational goals.

Top level Leadership must ensure the message is carefully delivered and then if the mid-level managers or supervisors are not 100% committed to implementing the change, then top-level management must decide if they, those mid-level managers or supervisors, are the right people, in the right place, at the right time.

If top level management fails to remedy this situation then Top-Level Leaders and stakeholders need to decide if they, *the top-level managers*, are the right people, in the right place, at the right time.

Change Management

Facilitating Change

Take careful consideration of each change individually. Plan the most appropriate approach to each situation. Then you need to analyze for *systemic issues* and areas for concurrent implementation opportunities … and train wrecks!

If you change *this* – how does it affect *that?*

HUH?

I mean, if you speed up the process, do you have enough warehouse space for all that extra stuff? (In the internet world – if your website goes viral – will it crash?)

No change will be successfully implemented without impacting additional areas of the organization.

Identify those other areas affected as early as possible in the change planning process. Untold treasures may be unearthed during open and frank discussions when analyzing impacts of the planned change.

When risk or opportunities are identified; it becomes an opportunity to improve the change plan. It is imperative to acknowledge the plan is just – the current plan – and it is a living and dynamic plan which must and shall evolve with the addition of new or better information.

Principles of Change

Understand and apply the principles, types and stages of change

and develop approaches to suit the situation.
Understand the tools, methodology and models to draw on when facilitating change.
Competently apply the behaviors and skill of leading change.

*Leadership of change involves the most unpredictable variable: **People**.*

Effectively leading change will require you to customize and scale your efforts based on the unique characteristics of the change and the attributes of your organization.

There is no secret formula!

Your strategy and approach must be designed according to your situation and you must constantly adjust your tactics to match the evolving conditions.

> 1. *Communications*
>> i. *Timely, constant, practical communications.*
> - *Leadership should communicate:*
>> ◦ *Why the change is necessary*
>> ◦ *The risk of not changing*
>> ◦ *How the change aligns with the organization's vision and business direction*
> - *Management should communicate:*
>> ◦ *How the change impacts the employee and their team*
>> ◦ *How the change affects their day-to-day responsibilities*
>> ◦ *What's in it for me?*
>> ◦ *What's in it for us (our team or workgroup)?*

Be clear in your communications.
Listen to understand how your message is being received.
Communicate repeatedly, and correct misinformation quickly!

> 2. *Resistance – Fear of the unknown*
>> ◦ *Resistance is expected, planning should be de-*

signed to mitigate resistance.
- ◦ *Manage resistance early and at its source.*
- ◦ *Engage your Team and build enthusiasm and passion around the change.*

3.   *Visible Leadership*

Are YOU in control of the stakeholders?

Does everyone see you as the Leader of the Change?
Do you have a strong coalition of other Leaders and Managers?

Are you committed to the Change? Or is there something else demanding your attention?

Are you LISTENING to your Team? Their ideas, their concerns?

If you have even one No in any of the above … you are not providing Leadership required for the Change.

THIS is the Point of Failure!

4.   *Values*

Understand the underlying values of your organization These factors directly influence the way change will be accepted and how much work will ultimately be required to ensure a successful outcome.

There is no magic formula for fully understanding your value systems.

Only after the strategy work is completed; can you customize and scale the specific change management action plans and consider the unique value systems of those impacted.

LISTEN!

5.   *Magnitude of change*
      The approach required is unique and specific to this change.

> *Adjust your approach based on how the change uniquely affects those impacted.*
> - *How big is the gap between the future state and the current state?*
> - *How different is the future state from the current state?*
> - *How much of a departure from the current state is the future state?*

A one-size-fits-all approach is not appropriate or effective. Understand the magnitude, disruption, gap and size of change to build the right approach.

6. *Your approach*
   > *Your solution must be adopted and embraced by everyone.*

7. *The Process*
   > *Change is a process ...not as a single event or series of events*
   > *Individuals experience change as a process.*
   > *Evaluate and focus on where individuals are in the change process.*
   > *No one experiences the process the same.*
   > *Your organizational efforts need to be tied to where the organization is in the process.*

8. *Prepare for the unexpected.*
   > *No change program goes completely according to plan!*

9. *People matter*
   > *Be as honest and explicit as possible*
   > *People will react to what they see and hear*

Highly visible rewards ... promotion, recognition, and bonuses ... provide dramatic reinforcement for embracing change.
Sanction or removal of people standing in the way of change will reinforce commitment.

10. *Improvement is a journey!*

You will not succeed all at once.
Strive for significant improvements – and REWARD them!

The Environment

Consider your organization's strategy, structure, process and culture when diagnosing change including organizational, individual, economic, cultural, social and political forces.
Remain open to ideas, support and use promising ideas to solve problems and address issues.

Promote and demonstrate active listening skills to identify the sources of resistance and anticipate concerns.

Business Focus

Use change as an opportunity to advance business objectives.
Recognize and effectively communicate and manage the business case for change – evaluate the costs and the benefits.

Change Readiness

Correctly assesses employees' readiness for the change then build the communication plan and messages accordingly and conduct regular reviews.

Reward efforts to change.

Work to minimize complexities, contradictions and paradoxes or reduce their impact.

Clarify direction and smooth the process of change.
Use the data gathered in change readiness and impact assessments to inform design, plan and implement activities and priorities.

Culture Awareness

Identify both the overt and covert culture of the organization and its influence on the change.

Design approach and plans with an awareness of prevailing cultures.

Strategic Thinking

The application of information on internal and external drivers for the change when scoping, planning and making decisions

Vision

Develop, reinforce and communicate a precise vision which understands the drivers for change in the organization's strategy.

Maintain a long term, strategic view of the change to identify risks and opportunities. Identify the width of the scope of change

Build communication strategy based on scope. Quickly assess the current and future context for a change.
Communicate the vision ... let Management manage the *How* ... YOU define the *Why*.

Assess Readiness

Regularly monitor organizational readiness for change. These are probably the six most ignored words in the book. Ignore them at your own peril.

Strategic View

Challenge the thinking and question assumptions ... but, do so in a constructive way.

Recognize likely impacts on business strategies and plans and discuss with your Team.

Correctly assess the impact of other changes and adapt an approach which exploits opportunities or take mitigation action as required.

Recognize the need for integration across multiple change programs and projects that will impact common stakeholders ... *(If this works in the Region X ... it should work in Region Y also.)*

Sustainable Outcome

Build for lasting solutions, owned by the entire organization, which take account of other current and future changes. (Including THIS one!)

Thinking and Judgement

Apply logic and thinking processes to analyses situations and problems to design effective solutions.

Demonstrate the capacity to reflect, analyses and develop workable frameworks and plans by incorporating other viewpoints in your process.

Analytical Thinking

Work systematically to resolve problems, identify causes, anticipate implications and make informed decisions, critically question information and use insights obtained to understand the situation.
Draw out the key issues to identify underlying trends and question your own assumptions.

Perspective

Maintain a big picture perspective, rather than only positional or functional viewpoints.

Consider broad potential consequences of decisions; identify *root cause* to problems and take appropriate action.

Decision Making

Make timely decisions; Set priorities based on adequate information ... a 70% plan implemented today beats a perfect plan implemented later – every time!

Develop comprehensive solutions and strategies – define the *Why* – leave the *How*-to Management.

Authenticity is more than speaking. Authenticity is also about doing. Every decision you make says something about who you are.

Influencing Others

The effective exploration of alternatives and positions to reach outcomes to gain all parties' support and acceptance.

A great idea is a great idea.

The art of getting others to see things as you see them ... persuasion ... is a key skill.

You must persuade the right people to implement your idea.

Provide a good reason to support your idea. State the loss not just the increase.

Tell a damn good story!

Customer/ Stakeholder Focus

Continually identify the stakeholders affected by the change, be sure to involve the right people at the right time by developing, maintaining and working with stakeholder engagement strategies and plans.

Proactively focuses on both internal and external stakeholders, by making efforts to understand their needs, gives high priority to stakeholder satisfaction. Obtain commitment through consultation and consideration of stakeholder impacts ... ensure all stakeholders are fairly represented.

Professional Presence

Always display a credible presence and positive image.

Develop other people's confidence in you through consistent action, values and communication.

Networking

Display your ability to influence outside of your own function and to form alliances with other areas, industries, functions and organizations.

Build networks and relationships of benefit to your team and your organization. Use your network to influence seemingly *unreachable* parties.

Interpersonal Style

Adopt appropriate interpersonal styles and techniques to gain acceptance of ideas or plans.

Modify your behavior to accommodate tasks, situations and individuals involved.

Identify and use sources of power, when needed, to help move forward.

> *Modify – Adopt. Again, this requires a deep awareness of the situation; modify does not mean to abandon your style – it means to incorporate those elements of the situation, you need to use to make others more receptive to your ideas and plans. If you are trying to influence a Japanese company you should attempt to use chopsticks ... don't just insist on a spoon or a fork. Simple things can build bridges in a relationship and is the foundation of respect and winning.*

Coaching for Change

Prepare your managers and employees for change through coaching in managing change skills and building your organizational capability for the future.

Adult Learning Principles

Understand and apply the principles of adult learning and coaching.

Change Management for Managers

Understand the principles of change management and coach managers in managing people in dealing with a changing environment.

Recognize the dual role of managers as recipients and implementers of change and takes an appropriate approach.

Coach people through change.

Needs Analysis

Conduct a diagnosis to identify the scope of change and prepare interventions, communication plans and training accordingly.

Organizational Capability

Uses coaching plans to increase overall organizational capability in managing change.

Role Model

Act as a role model for others, shares knowledge and coach others.

Champion New Skills

Provide appropriate training and workplace learning opportunities to provide for the development of any necessary new skills and which support the goals of the change initiative.

The following is an overview of Management's focus. It is included as a reminder to Leaders to *Lead* and NOT Manage.

Enable your Management Team through effective Leadership!

Project Management

The application of knowledge, skills, tools and techniques to project activities to meet or exceed stakeholder needs and expectations from the project

Plan Development

Prepare an integrated plan for change management, defining the governance, scope, milestones, deliverables, outcomes, benefits and due dates – *these are the How's!*

Prepare a schedule showing detailed tasks, dependencies, skills, effort, start/finish dates and resources required to achieve the outcomes

Consider possible constraints when selecting options for the plan: resource availability, timing, organizational capabilities, readiness, costs and staff attitude towards the change

Get agreements on success measures, key milestones and dates

Define change stream structure with roles and responsibilities of all participants clearly documented

Monitor and Management of Progress

Communicate progress to all stakeholders regularly, using relevant factual data in an objective, understandable format

Adjust plan in response to changing needs and effectively communicates changes

Review progress by collecting objective data and taking corrective action where required Understand the roles and relationships of the project manager, project team and other stakeholders and can competently manage those relationships

Understand team dynamics and how this affects working relationships at various stages.

Cost Management

Accurately estimate the costs incurred for change management activities.
Effectively source, manage, report against and work to an agreed budget.

Risk and Opportunity Management

Evaluate and balance risk exposure in developing and implementing an approach.

Identify and quantify potential risks, monitor and manage them throughout the project.

Vendor Management

Build constructive relationships with external vendors ensuring clear roles and responsibilities.

Initiate and maintain contractual conditions and relationships.

Review Project Outcomes

Review and report on outcomes and success measures (benefits) at each milestone.

Use learnings to enhance effectiveness for the future.

Communication Skills

The building and maintaining of open, collaborative and reciprocal relationships with others.

Relationship Building

Create and maintain value added relationships

Understand collaboration and how to develop it in relationships

Apply principled negotiation to achieve win/win outcomes in dealings with others

Actively support teamwork through collaboration and effective relationships

Build rapport and keep others in the loop
Facilitate the discussion of conflicting issues between individuals and groups

Collaborate with others, seek and utilize feedback

Oral Communication

Express ideas effectively in individual and group situations; adjusts language to the characteristics and needs of the audience.

Use open questions and active listening to ensure individuals/situations are clearly understood.

Written Communication

Express ideas clearly in documents which have organization, structure, grammar, language and terminology adjusted to the characteristics and needs of the audience.

Measures Effectiveness of Communication

Regularly measure the effectiveness of communication and adjusts approach accordingly.

Plan communication which is clear about purpose, desired outcomes, key messages and audience needs.

Use the expertise of subject matter experts when designing

communications and presentations.

Plan

Plans, documents and gains agreement to the approach to communication.

Communications Strategies - Solution Design and Development

Use the appropriate communication style and media for the situation and audience.

Work with key stakeholders to create most appropriate communications.

Empathy

Be attentive to cues (e.g. body language), and respond appropriately.

Demonstrate empathy, relate to people and listen to their viewpoints.

Use empathy to consider stakeholder views, plan stakeholder engagement, plan and prioritizes activities and tailor communication materials.

Self-Management

Take full accountability for own performance in achieving change management outcomes.

Personal Responsibility

Assume accountability for own role, consistently aiming for high performance.

Accept responsibility for own choices, actions, non-actions, successes and failures.

Understand personal limitations and seek expertise for assistance where this would benefit the outcome.

Set challenging goals and take calculated risks.

Prioritization and Time Management

Juggle the priorities of multiple activities and stakeholders to meet diverse and sometimes conflicting deadlines.

Maintain clear focus on goal achievement, confront problems, conflicts and obstacles.

Resilience

Stay focused under pressure!

Deal with setbacks and bounce back from failure, learn from experience and adjust behavior where necessary.

Flexibility

Modify behavior to deal effectively with changes in the work environment, try innovative approaches appropriate for new or changed situations, do not persist with ineffective behaviors.

Remain focused during periods of ambiguity.

Emotional Intelligence

Understand the impact your actions have on others and adjust approach where necessary.

Expresses emotions appropriately.

Consider people's feelings when making decisions.

Respond to emotions in others.

Facilitation – Meetings and Workshops Design

Consider the broad context for the event when preparing design

Have a straightforward vision of the purpose and outcomes of the session – agreed with the client if appropriate

Plan relevant group exercises, methods and processes to deliver the desired outcomes

Allocate time appropriately, realistically and effectively

Participatory Environment

Create and sustain a participatory environment to gain involvement/participation of group members

Take account of distinctive styles and provide opportunities for all group members to get involved

Take a position of neutrality regarding content to maximize involvement, trust and openness
Understand team development and group dynamics and ensure an environment of two-way expressive involvement

Structure

Provide structure to meetings and workshops in terms of agenda, discussions, decision making, format and physical environment arrangement

Take responsibility for developing, communicating and monitoring and maintaining structure of session

Process

Employ a range of facilitation tools for use in planning, identifying issues and potential solutions

Monitor the event to ensure agreed outcomes and timelines will be met

Tactfully refocuses the group back to the session purpose and agenda item when needed

Understand your own limits and takes care not to take the group into inappropriate (highly emotional) territory

Understand when a group member's behavior is impacting results, also when they have the capabilities to act in the most appropriate manner to support

Bring events to closure by summarizing actions, decisions, time frames and responsibilities

Professional Development

A continual effort to gain more knowledge, develop more effective skills and promote the profession of change management

Knowledge

Proactively seeks out new and up-to-date information which can be applied

Assess and integrate new knowledge

Skills

Seek feedback as input to professional development plan

Focus skill development on under developed areas.

Integrates new skills and seeks out opportunities to apply new skills

Find opportunities to build new skills through both formal and informal channels

Promotion of Change Management

Provide simple explanations of the distinct aspects of change management to educate

Specialist Expertise

The high-level assessment of needs, approaches, design and delivery methods for the implementation of solutions

Learning & Development

Needs Identification

Ensure the learning and development needs of each group impacted by change are identified

Training Plan

Work with subject matter experts to ensure appropriate training plans are in place for all stakeholders

Ensure change management project plan reflects all steps for the delivery of training

Solution Delivery

Ensure implementation plans are in place for training rollouts to all impacted stakeholders
Monitor the rollout of training for all stakeholders, according to the project management plan
Manage the process of requirements, design and delivery of solution
Monitor the development and delivery of communication solutions and reports on progress

Evaluation

Take steps to evaluate effectiveness
Ensure results of training are evaluated and report to

other stakeholders

Analyses the results of evaluation and takes required action

Needs Identification

Identify the communications needs of each stake-holder group impacted by change

Resistance to Organizational Change

Resistance to organizational change is just one of the impediments to organizational expansion and growth.

The point of failure ... Is Leadership's failure to share influence with those of unequal hierarchy.

Once again, I stress **Leadership's failure.**

Leadership's commitment to the change will be undermined by Managers who fail to embrace those ideas and concerns of Team members. Leadership must require Managers to clearly document and report the inclusion of all stakeholders (and THIS means all Team members!) and their concerns are fairly represented.

This is a critical to success factor!

Thinking and Judgement

Apply logic and analytical thinking to find effective solutions.

Irrational ideas and emotions are key contributors to the failure of the Change initiative.

Irrational ideas are just ... irrational. The higher the level of an irrational idea, then higher the level of resistance. Simple math. Irrational ideas need for Leadership to apply logic and insightful thinking.

Let's break it down:

Logically address the idea. Duh! Of course! BUT, how do you address an idea? Through effective listening! Ideas may be expressed as concerns. Ideas may also be expressed as alternatives. Sometimes are expressed as ... ideas! Wow! Could it really be that simple? Yes and no. the expression is a symptom. The symptom is an indicator of the direction needed for effective questioning. By asking effective questions ... consecutively and focused on determining the underlying cause of the irrational idea, you will be able to correctly identify – and confirm – the true issue. An effective solution addresses the root cause – not the symptom!

Analytical Thinking

Systematically to resolve problems, identify causes, anticipate implications and make informed decisions Critically question information, use insights to understand the situation
Identify key issues and underlying trends
Reflects and questions own assumptions

Perspective

Maintain a *big picture* perspective; consider consequences of decisions.

It is important to also consider *unintended consequences*. Here too it is paramount to success the participation of those with skin in the game are included in discussions. Their intimate insights will help reveal situations and effects which may not be readily apparent.

Identify *root causes*, take appropriate action

Decision Making

Makes timely decisions. Set priorities based on available information.

NOTE: **Decide!** Adjust the implementation plan. Monitor and measure.
Complexity makes decision-making more challenging, regardless of company size.
Decisions you make with integrity are the ones you can sleep with.
Seek input from others — *especially those who think differently from you* — understand how to filter and synthesize the insights you receive
Have enough context to make an informed decision.

Three core principles:
- Pay attention to *instincts*, listen to your *gut*.
- Exercise *judgment* – draw on data and experiences to reach conclusions.
- Use the *perspectives* of peers, mentors and employees to inform—but do not dictate— decisions.

Ensure the decision aligns with the mission, vision and purpose.
Develop your own process, unique for you. It's important to develop a model that feels authentic to you. What counts is you rigorously apply a conscious process leading to better decisions — and better results for you and your firm.

When a project is in trouble

- Identify potential issues early; determine the best course of action to address them quickly.

- Systemic problems need systemic solutions.
- Solve the problems by planning, sequencing tasks, and co-ordination among cross functional groups. **Few projects meet this standard.**
- Collaborative problem solving is essential to reduce variability.
- Focus on meeting milestones and *do not underestimate* the effort required.

Ali Esshaq

Addendum

The Rules ...

> Points Not Covered by Rules
>> If any point in dispute is not covered by the Rules, the decision *should be made in accordance with equity.*

Read that again. Should be *The Rules of Life.*

It Starts at the Top

Change is hard and without Leadership from the top, impossible.

I don't think it's improbable the organization will change. I think it's impossible!

Without your Leadership from the top your company won't change, and your company definitely will not become any more innovative.

Often Leaders think if they send their people to workshops, what's being taught will magically be instituted at their company. If you think this is going to magically happen in your company you are sadly mistaken.

Far too many organizations continue to make the mistake of focusing too much on business processes and not enough on good, strong examples of Leadership.

If you're the Leader and you don't do the challenging work of leading the change, it's just not going to happen. It's nice you can send your employees to great programs on how to be more innovative, create niches, or make your company lean. If you don't learn what it's all about and understand the challenges in making changes real ... then those changes won't ever get off the ground.

The problem in creating something new is there is too much inertia against change even if the change is for the better. You must be very clear about what's going to happen and give Leadership to those making changes.

I've noticed when Leaders don't have a clear understanding of what the goals of change are, **changes won't happen**. This means to have meaningful changes and implementation of innovative ideas; you will have to lead! If you're not willing lead, you are wasting your money and the time of your people.

Change only happens when Leadership is intimately involved. Without your participation you just waste time, money, and effort.

Building your ability as a Leader is the first step in the change management process. Once your Team believes in you and trust what you're doing, you can then begin your campaign for change.

- *Be the Example*
- *Communicate*
- *Be You! - one-to-one basis, build rapport, trust and confidence.*
- *Be Passionate! Leadership is tiring and saps energy at a very high rate so make sure you are passionate about what you do.*

NOTE: It is important you realize you will never be able to implement without experiencing at least some resistance. People adjust to change at different rates. It's just part of human nature. To reduce your frustration with this process, you need to be aware of the six phases people go through whenever they are experiencing any type of change, be it personal or professional.

1. Anticipation. People don't know what to expect so they wait, anticipating what the future holds.
2. Confrontation. They are beginning to realize the change is really going to happen or is happening.
3. Realization. They realize nothing is ever going to be as it once was.
4. Depression. Your Team mourns the past. Not only have they realized the change intellectually, but now they are beginning to comprehend it emotionally as well. *This is a critical-to-success factor!*
5. Acceptance. Your Team begins to accept the change emotionally. Although they may still have reservations,

they are not fighting the change at this stage. Usually, they are beginning to see some of the benefits even if they are not completely convinced.

6. Enlightenment. Your Team completely accept the new change. In fact, many wonder how they ever managed the *old way*. Overall, they feel good about the change and accept it as the status quo from here forward.

It is important to note people in your organizations will proceed through the distinct phases at different rates of speed. Communications is extremely important throughout the process.

Strong Leadership and frequent communication are always important, but they are crucial during the change process. What is important with respect to Leadership communication is it be frequent and forthright, answering the questions your people are asking.

(Back to Topic)

Transformational Leadership

Changing your organization is a challenge. How would you like to change the world? Well, it has already been accomplished … several times. One person can change the world. 100 people that changed the world.

I'll use FDR as an example.

Challenges:

1. Elected during the height of the Great Depression;
    a. Facing an unprecedented economic crisis;
2. World War Two;
    a. Promised to stay out of World War Two;
    b. Entered World War Two whole-heartedly;

FDR came from a privileged background; however, recognized the importance of helping less fortunate people.

Changes:

Facing an unprecedented economic crisis: FDR implemented changes at the top through hands-on Leadership. Programs like WPA and CCC employed thousands. Priming the economy. Individual States were not equipped to deal with such massive programs. FDR CHANGED the status quo to a Federally led status. His personal commitment was a driving factor.

Promised to stay out of World War Two: American had a long history of *isolationism*. During the 1930s, the combination of the Great Depression and the memory of tragic losses in World War I contributed to pushing American public opinion and policy toward isolationism (source)

Entered WW II whole-heartedly: FDR Leadership and personal commitment were driving forces to implement the changes required at the country's highest levels and impacted the world.

These examples clearly demonstrate effective change – **transformational change** – may be accomplished at any level. Common to both is the **LEADER'S** personal commitment to the change.

> "I'm not the smartest fellow in the world, but I can sure pick smart colleagues."   ***FDR***

Isolationism*:   A policy of remaining apart from the affairs or interests of other groups, especially the political affairs of other countries.*

Resistance to organizational change is just one of the impediments to organizational expansion and growth.

Factors such as lack of motivation, poor channels of communication, and information exchange also contribute to resistance. This suggests management should encourage employee participation to build confidence in the process, accept constructive criticism, be transparent and communicate clearly the benefits of the change to employees.

Background

Organizations operate within an increasingly volatile environment, in a state of constant change. The pressure to change stems from a variety of internal and external sources such as political, economic, social, technological and market factors. Organizational change is aimed at adapting to the environment, improvement in performance and changes in employees' behavioral patterns at the work place. For the sake of survival, growth, and having a competitive advantage. Organizations have attempted to anticipate and adapt to changes through strategies including organizational redesign, which often embodies changes to the very culture of the organization.

Even though change is implemented for positive reasons (to adapt to changing environmental conditions and remain competitive), employees often respond negatively toward change and resist the change efforts. This negative reaction is largely because change brings with its increased pressure, stress and uncertainty for employees. The reasons for the failure to effectively implement the needed change range from a lack of understanding surrounding an organization's capacity for change to other human factors, such as employee resistance toward organizational change. Numerous studies indicating resistance to change as the most frequent problem faced by management in implementing change.

Organizational change, in this context, is defined as ~ *a reconfiguration of an organization to increase efficiency and effectiveness.*

Resistance to change may be defined as *Employee action or inaction which is intended to avoid a change and/or interfere with the successful implementation of a change in its current form.*

If resistance to change is properly managed, by the top-level management team, then it helps to challenge and refine the strategy and action plans and improves the quality of decision making.

3 take-aways:

Change – transparency
      Tell the truth
      Tell them you will find out for them
      Tell them you cannot tell them

Communications –

      Stay ahead of the rumor mill

Let 'em vent!

      When YOU hear it first hand – then you can effectively deal with the issue!

Build others
      Never criticize
         Focus on solving the issue

      Never complain
      Never appear as a victim
      Actively discuss the issue –
      Solve the issue

      Never Condemn

      It will come back on you! Guaranteed!

Never disagree

Discuss, listen, then decide

Think ~ *It isn't right or wrong – it is a difference in opinion.*
I may be right this time or I may be wrong, we will see.
If I am right, okay, if I am wrong okay. However, this is my responsibility and I have made my decision.

I may not be wrong on this, but certainly I will be wrong at some time. That is why I value your insights and I always want to hear your opinions and input. You make me better.

The Purple Book

*Congratulations on taking another step to becoming a **Champion!***

Your purchase of The Purple Book demonstrates you are a forward-thinking Leader and value critical insights!

With your purchase, you have become a member of a very select few who have chosen to pursue a passion for excellence. I value your comments and insights ... so send them to me!

Whenever you are feeling *stuck* just search for a related topic for additional information.

My intention in writing *My Purple Book* is to provide you with a *nudge* in the right direction. You may find the inspiration you need ... or even that *missing piece-of-the-puzzle*.

However, if you need a helping hand or just want someone to bounce an idea off ... contact me. I will help you get *unstuck!*

Semper Fi,

Ali

'*Who is this for?*'
> Leaders requiring access to immediate guidance for their most pressing Challenges!

'*What does this do?*'
> *Provides an insight on a specific topic where the busy Executive needs to get a Kick-Start on direction. Help to stimulate thoughtful consideration.*

'*Does it have a purpose?*'
> *Helps in decision making through providing insightful information.*

'*Does it add value to the world?*'
> **Hell, YES!**

'*How will it improve the lives of the people who buy it?*'
> *By helping Leaders become better Leaders and winners to be*

Champions!

My Purple Book

Expands on each topic found in *The Little Purple Book* and provides access to valuable insights to help the busy Executive. Based on over 50 years of practical experience solving unique challenges on engagements around the world.

My Purple Book

Is evolving, constantly changing and continuously updated resource! To ensure that you have the current version with the latest up-to-date information:

Register your copy to receive free updates as soon as they are available.

Credits:

I am an avid reader and researcher; therefore, I am constantly reading articles from those who I find value in their work. I may not always agree with their opinions, BUT I always value their opinions.

It is without a doubt, I have included some of their thoughts (and language!) into my writing … whether I gave credit in the context or not; I do give credit to all of those who have influenced my thoughts and by such, my writing.

Disclaimer:

Neither the United States Marine Corps nor any other component of the Department of Defense has approved, endorsed, or authorized this content.

Thanks for the inspiration (and credit!) to:

The **United States Marine Corps**

My Father. 1926 to 1985.
Served in the United States Navy 1940.
Served in the United States Marine Corps 1940 to 1969.

The Commandant of the Marine Corps ~ *General Robert B. Neller*

Sergeant Major of the Marine Corps ~ *Sergeant Major Ronald L. Green*

Lt. Gen. Lewis *Chesty* Puller ~ June 26, 1898 ~ October 11, 1971

General James Mattis

Monroe R. Meyerson 1930 - 2008
Sidney Milgrim 1924 – 2007

Lt. Gen. Lewis *Chesty* Puller

Chesty Puller is the most decorated Marine in American history.

"Old breed? New breed? There is not a damn bit of difference so long as it is Marine breed."

> *Breed* ~ "Having a distinctive appearance and typically having been developed by deliberate selection."

My take … A Marine is a distinctive "Breed."

"Don't forget that you're First Marines! Not all the Communists in hell can overrun you!"

"You don't hurt 'em if you don't hit 'em."

"Hit hard, hit fast, hit often."

"Where the Hell do you put the bayonet?"
(He said this while at a flamethrower demonstration. Apparently, Puller wanted to be ready to stab the men he set on fire.)

"All right. They're on our left, they're on our right, they're in front of us, they're behind us … they can't get away this time."

"Great. Now we can shoot at those bastards from every direction."

"All right you bastards, try and shoot me."

"There are not enough china men in the world to stop a fully armed Marine regiment from going where ever they want to go."

"We make generals today on the basis of their ability to write a damned letter. Those kinds of men can't get us ready for war."

"Son, when the Marine Corps wants you to have a wife, you will be issued one."

(This was Puller's response to a young Marine who was asking permission to be married.)

General James Mattis

"You cannot allow any of your people to avoid the brutal facts. If they start living in a dream world, it's going to be bad."

"If in order to kill the enemy you have to kill an innocent, don't take the shot. Don't create more enemies than you take out by some immoral act."

"I come in peace. I didn't bring artillery. But I'm pleading with you, with tears in my eyes: If you fuck with me, I'll kill you all."

"The first time you blow someone away is not an insignificant event. That said, there are some a--holes in the world that just need to be shot. There are hunters and there are victims. By your discipline, you will decide if you are a hunter or a victim."

"Be polite, be professional, but have a plan to kill everybody you meet."

"We've backed off in good faith to try and give you a chance to straighten this problem out. But I am going to beg with you for a minute. I'm going to plead with you, do not cross us. Because if you do, the survivors will write about what we do here for 10,000 years."

"I don't lose any sleep at night over the potential for failure. I cannot even spell the word."

"There are some people who think you have to hate them in order to shoot them. I don't think you do. It's just business."

"Marines don't know how to spell the word defeat."

"The most important 6 inches on the battlefield is between your ears."

"In this age, I don't care how tactically or operationally brilliant you are, if you cannot create harmony — even vicious harmony — on the battlefield based on trust across service lines, across coalition and national lines, and across civilian/military lines, you need to go home, because your Leadership is obsolete. We have got to have officers who can create harmony across all those lines."

"Treachery has existed as long as there's been warfare, and there's always been a few people that you couldn't trust."

"You are part of the world's most feared and trusted force. Engage your brain before you engage your weapon."

"For the mission's sake, for our country's sake, and the sake of the men who carried the Division's colors in past battles — 'who fought for life and never lost their nerve' — carry out your mission and keep your honor clean.

Demonstrate to the world there is *'No Better Friend — No Worse Enemy'* than a US Marine."

When everything is at stake, your Leadership, is the most important factor. Determining whether you, your Team and your organization succeeds or fails.

The Little Purple Book provides insights into those tough Leadership lessons. Tips, but no tricks. Developed to help you build your own high-performance Teams and lead them.

The 14 Leadership Principles and 11 Traits. That enable you to improvise, adapt and overcome!

An entertaining narrative with powerful instructions and direct applications.

Intended to help you to fulfill your ultimate purpose:

Lead and Win.

Arab Leaders

Arab Leaders will have to muster the unity, vision, and courage to lift their countries up by their bootstraps.

When was the last time Arabs held a summit to produce a vision and action plan for how they're going to improve their countries?

Arab Human Development Reports (AHDR), written by Arab scholars and researchers, catalogue the failure of Arabs to build societies based on freedom, good governance, and respect for human dignity. They also offer solid recommendations for reforms.

Arab Leaders should be leading this charge ...

You are leading in a time of the transition from the merchant family to the corporate society. You are a Leader in a first-generation corporate society. That makes you unique.

This transition is not a new concept. You can learn from other regions that made this transition to see how it is done.

Exploring the early 20th century, *the time of creation of the corporate society,* for insights on leading in the Middle East, is far more valuable than looking at current business models.

While the corporate society reality may be new to the Middle East, its rise from the original family business and government-sector model in other areas can provide clues towards what your business should be doing.

The Middle East boasts only a few mature family businesses and some go back generations. Most people in the current workforce are among the first members from their family to work in a corporate environment. They have historically worked in the public sector or small neighborhood-style businesses. Only recently have they started to work in a corporate setting.

One of the challenges is the need to build social support and development systems for a corporate environment. The *old way* of doing business, based on family relationships, will not take your business to the next level.

We are leaping to a corporate society, but without having decades of corporate practices built into our society. In industrialized nations, business structures come from a systematic mentality, while in the Middle East business structures come from family orientation.

One important thing is for Leaders to open their eyes to the specific demands and expectations of employees, most of whom are from a first-generation corporate society and, unfortunately, may be lacking in those basic corporate skills required to effectively contribute.

This is vital information for anyone leading an organization here.

Understanding and using this information will enable you to adapt your Leadership approach to whoever you are leading and is critical to the success of your organization.

www.ingramcontent.com/pod-product-compliance
Lightning Source LLC
Chambersburg PA
CBHW030728180526
45157CB00008BA/3084